This Book Belongs

_____

52 SUNDAYS

A keepsake collection of
Letters from God

LESLIE C. DOBSON

ISBN: 978-0-9687047-3-8 (Paperback)

RELIGION, CHRISTIAN LIVING, INSPIRATIONAL
AND PERSONAL GROWTH, SPIRITUAL GROWTH

Dedication

This book is dedicated to all the people, who throughout my life, have shared their light with me, thank you. It is through you that I am able to see God's work in the world.

Prologue

This book is a compilation of blogs written and posted each Sunday by Leslie over the course of year. It is recommended that you set aside a small amount of time one day a week, read one letter and then sit in quiet reflection with God in prayer.

Before sitting down to write a Letter from God, Leslie always sat in silent prayer and asked God to send her His words for His children. The ask always was, and will continue to be, that it be His words and that they reach whoever needs them most. It is with that same intent that this book is being created.

This collection was a calling from God; a silent whisper to become a messenger of light and love. Everyone will take something different from each letter depending on where they are at in their life's journey.

Whatever may have brought this book into your hands, may you hear the voice of God and feel His love around you always. Never forget that being His makes you special. Wherever you may wander in this life may you always let your light shine.

Table of Contents

Be Patient With One Another

Remember, you are perfect in my eyes, you are not flawed. Your scars, the colour of your eyes, your hair, your skin, is what makes you who you are. Look at my fruit; each one similar and yet of many different wonderful varieties. You are my fruit! You are beautiful! You are special!

When a child is pulled away by their curiosity, encourage them, let them explore safely. Plan time for this in your day. It will remind you of who you were once, and how beautiful and exciting the world can be. Watch them as they learn with joy. Teach them right from wrong, to love and not hate; to be ever happily curious about life and all the treasures it holds.

When your elder walks slower, or takes longer to explain something, be patient. Give them time. They have earned it with their years of living. When they tell you a story, listen, for they are the history keepers of the world. They have a knowledge of life that cannot always be found in your books. They have life lessons to teach and pass on.

Cherish them as I do, for you will not have them always.

I have much more to say to you my children, but that is for another day. Until then, know this – I love you, you are special, you are my children. Be kind and loving and patient with one another.

I Am With You

I am with you my children. You are not alone. I know you do not always see me, or hear me, but I am there; standing right beside you with my hand on your shoulder. You, are as much a part of me, as I am of you. I will never leave you.

I come to you in many ways, shapes and forms, although you do not always recognize me. I come to you on the wind, in the lyrics of a song, in a picture or image that you might notice as you drive by. I am there with you, guiding you, loving you always, if only you'd let me.

If you quiet your mind and your thoughts and ask with the confidence of knowing I will answer; you will find what it is you are seeking. You will know what the answer is and in which direction you are to go.

At times, I come in the form of a friend who shows up or calls at just the right time. Other times, I am the thought in your head urging you to take action and perform deeds of kindness; to call a friend or loved one who is struggling. When you do that and act out of love, you yourself are me, you represent me on my behalf and I work through you.

I see so many of you struggling, hurting, questioning. Do not give up, do not quit, for I am there. I am with you and will never leave you. If the world around you is too heavy, hand it over to me to hold for a little while so you can rest.

I am here, I am ever waiting, ever listening and ever loving. I am with you and I will never leave you.

Be A Light To Others

Shine your light outward my children, shine it for all to see. Be a light to others, a beacon in their storm. You are the measuring stick, not the measurer. You need to shine your light and walk in faith so that others may see and be able to follow. You can lead them out of darkness, out of loneliness, out of pain just by sharing your light with them.

I did not entrust you with the light of the Spirit for it to stay housed in your shell, but rather for you to shine that light outward; out into the world where others are dwelling in the shadows and the darkness. Light dispels the dark, casts the shadows away; that is the job I have entrusted to you. That, is the job you were made for. You were made to shine, so shine, shine brightly, shine always!

Your light will not diminish when you use it, rather I will continue to replenish it. Your light will shine brighter and all will know that you are a beacon, a disciple of faith and of love, of kindness and of hope. Shine my children, shine.

Walk away from the shadows and stand in the light, share the light, embrace the light. Shed the skin of pain and sorrow, loneliness and hurt and embrace the warmth that the light has to offer, the love that is within the light. I am here, I am the light, you are of me, you are the light.

Be the light for others and shine, shine, shine! Shine bright my children, shine bright. In every day, in everything you do, shine!

Be Patient My Children

Be patient my children; patient with yourself, your loved ones, with your friends, and those people you may not yet know. Remember that although you may not know them intimately, the strangers are your brothers and sisters through me, they also need your patience.

While you do not always know what is happening in their life, I do. I see the worries, the hurt, the pain, their joy and I know why they are rushed or gruff at times. I see your pain, your joy, and I am here for you as I am for them. I can comfort you and celebrate with you if you will let me.

Know that I am not done with you yet. You must hang on and be patient. Things will happen when they are meant to, and when you need them to. Sometimes when you go through hard times it is for a reason, although you cannot see it. Do not give up, be patient and keep working. Keep being kind, loving and considerate; be patient in all you do.

Be patient with love my children. Remember that no one is perfect all the time. People will make mistakes, loved ones will make mistakes, you will make mistakes in love, so you must be patient with them and yourself. Do not rush love for it to unfolds when and as it needs.

You are a work of art, my work, my masterpiece in progress. I continually mold and shape you so that you can be the best possible version of yourself. I spend a long time and put all my love and care into my work because you are mine, my precious child.

Occasionally, you decide you do not like how things are going and you cast me aside or change my work, scribbling over my masterpiece with your impatient crayons. You are free to do that but know I will still be here, patiently waiting for you to return, patiently waiting to continue working on and with my masterpiece.

Be patient my children, for I am not finished with you yet.

Forgive Each Other

Forgive each other, my children. Stop hurting each other and stop holding fast to the hurts.

You must forgive even the harshest of hurts against you. I know it can be hard at times to do this. I know that when you are hurting it can turn to anger against the one that hurt you. After all, how dare they do this to you? I need you to forgive their sins my child. I know it is hard but you must do this for me. It is a journey you must take, a step you must climb.

No one is perfect and some are struggling more than you know. Often others hurt you so they are not alone in their pain. This is wrong! They should not act in such a way; however, it is not them I am talking to at the moment, it is you. Forgive them. Do not put yourself in the same situation, to be hurt over and over again, but do forgive them and move on.

Anger is darkness. If you let the anger boil over into your heart, and do not forgive, the one who has harmed you wins. Anger will tear your world and your family apart. It will fester and impact every area of your life, even when you don't want it to. You must forgive so this does not happen. Pass your pain on to me, I can bear it my child. I can hold it for you. I am here.

Do Not Judge One Another

Do not judge one another my children. That job is not yours, it is mine and mine alone. You can never know the full story of a person's life.

You do not always see their struggles, their pain and their sorrow. I see this fully. I know what they are doing and what they are not. There is nothing they can hide from me.

When you judge another, you are placing yourself above them. You are not better, or worse, than they are. You are different and unique, and I love you.

You have your own faults, your own mistakes, and your own troubles to bear. I would not have them judge you, nor would you want them to. Would you want to have every single moment of your life laid bare for them to judge you? I know you do not, so why then do you feel you are better than they, and able to judge them?

When you judge another person, you are saying you know better. One can always offer advice to another when you see they are struggling. That is not judging, that is helping. That is okay my children.

Helping and loving each other is what I want you to do. What I do not want is for you to sit back and judge each other harshly.

Live and lead by example my children, this is how others will learn. This is how others will see me through you. Love one another my children, do not judge one another.

You Are All My Children

You are all my children and I love you, the sinner and saint alike. I know that no one is perfect but I am asking you to try to be the best person that you can be. A child of light and of love, of kindness and compassion. I love you, I will guide you if you let me. I will heal your hurts and your pain if you allow me to.

Just like any child growing, there is a process of learning. You are still young my children, and therefore you are still learning. You do not always hear my message or learn the lessons meant for you, therefore I repeat them until you do.

Like a child learning to walk, you must try and try again. I know that you will fall, but I am there to catch you, to guide you until you learn what you need to … then we will move on to the next lesson.

The enemy is at large in the world and he is using many of my children. I love all my children; you are all mine. I cannot help you if you walk away from me but I am always there waiting for you to return.

My angels are fighting battles for you that you cannot even see, they too are there for you. The enemy will not win but as he gets closer to losing he will try even harder. Do not give in to him, do not lose hope, for all is not lost. Know that I am hard at work and the battle will not be lost. In the end, the enemy is the only one who will lose.

You will grow in heart, soul and spirit my children as you each evolve. That is the way of the world and the spirit. As you grow in love and kindness your light will shine out for others. You will become a guide, someone that others can learn from. Know this and accept it with an open heart.

The world will see me through your actions, make them ones based in love and love alone. If you do this, then the world will truly know me.

I love you, you are all my children, and one day we will be together again.

I Have Sent You Angels

I have sent you angels my children. I have been sending you angels throughout your life and I will continue to do so.

Some of my angels you cannot see, while others you can as they are earthbound; angels meant to help, nurture, protect and heal. There are all kinds of angels available to you in your time of need.

Everyone has a different need which is why I have sent many earthbound angels to help you my children. Watch, listen, look and you will notice them. They are the ones who touch your heart so deeply you cannot but help to be drawn to them. They give you strength and help you fend off any demons that come across your path. They help you find peace in the most difficult of situations.

I will never leave you alone my children. I am with you; my angels are with you. Seek them out, they are there for you. Talk to the ones you cannot see, they will hear you.

When it comes time for me to call one of my angels' home, don't be angry with me my children. They have fulfilled their purpose and come home to rest and find peace. They are still there for you and will hear you when you talk to them. Some will even leave signs for you so that you know they are near.

Whatever you are going through children, know that my angels are with you … today, tomorrow, always.

Talk To Me

Talk to me my children, I am here and I am listening. I want to talk with you, listen to you, smile with you, after all you are my children.

Don't just come to me when things go wrong, or you need something. Tell me your joys, share your day and your dreams as well as your sadness. I see it all, but I am still a father just wanting his children to talk to him.

Talk to me in prayer, in song or just say 'hey God, what's up?' I'll hear you. I do answer you, although you do not always see or hear it. Your spirit knows the answer and will reveal it if you listen, and when the time is right. Sometimes you hear it but don't like my answer so you ignore it, hoping it will change, trying for another answer. The answer won't change, it is what it is because I love you.

Long have I waited my children for you to come to me with everything. As a new child you did, even though you don't remember. It was natural for you because you were innocent, not yet wanting to control everything. The funny thing is you cannot control everything, yet still you try.

Share your burdens with me my children. Your fears and sadness can all be borne by me. I am willing to carry them for you. A heavy burden is always lighter when carried by two rather than one.

I am your trusted confident. Your secrets are safe with me. No one will ever know the things you say to me. I am a safe place, a true friend and confident … a parent.

Talk to me my children, I am listening.

A Shelter From The Storm

I will give you shelter my children, a place to take refuge and be safe. In me you can rest.

All through your life there will be shelter, although not always physical and not always seen. I will keep you safe from the unseen battles that rage against you. My love for you will act as a dome, a shield, protecting you from the dark ravages that are occurring around you. My angels are also providing safety for you from the unseen darkness.

After death, there is a place to live, a shelter for all eternity where pain does not exist and only joy and love reside. I provide many kinds of shelter for all my children and all my animals.

I have also provided you with the tools to build your own shelter to keep you safe. Build your shelters strong and sturdy so that they will withstand the worst of storms.

Be safe my children, your soul is also in your house, provide it with a sturdy shelter as well. Keep your body strong, and let faith be your shield. You have all the armour you need to keep you safe when the storm finally comes.

You will have a final resting place with me. When those days come, your shelter will last forever, and can never be destroyed.

In me, my children, you will have a shelter from the storm.

Come A Little Closer

Come closer to me my children, I will not harm or hurt you. I am here for you, just come a little nearer each day and you will see. Do not turn away just because you cannot always hear my voice, I am here and I am listening.

Every time you pray, you come closer. Every good deed you do, you come closer. Every time you give pure, true love, you come closer.

The more my children pray and come closer to me, the harder the angel of darkness will work to steal you away. You will be safe in my care. When you come close to me I can protect you, but if you choose to walk away I cannot. You see my child, the choice is always yours, it has always been yours. Only you get to decide which path you will walk.

The angel of darkness is working harder than ever before. This is evident in the increase in crime, terrorism, profanity, adultery and violence. These things are rapidly growing, you must come closer and turn away for darkness will dissipate in the light.

The enemy makes temptation look easy and fun but you will find in the end it is not. It will not fulfill you and often you will only see this after you made the choice to walk away. Stand strong my children, do not be tempted.

Remember always that I love you my children. I am here, ever waiting for you to come a little closer to me.

Be Still

Be still my children. You are rushing around, all the time from one thing to the next. You cannot hear me when you are so busy doing everything else.

You seem restless, as if you cannot sit still and enjoy the beauty of what is around you; the glory of all things I have provided for you. Sit awhile and enjoy the beauty of this world.

When you are still my children you will find your center and can communicate with me. I hear you at all times, but, when you are rushing and busy you do not hear me. I want you to hear me my children, I want to spend time with you.

Be still child and I will be in your presence; I am all living things around you. Be still and watch for me, listen for me. I am the child that laughs in the sprinklers, I am the smile on an old woman's face, I am the gentle breeze that caresses your face, I am the tired soul living homeless on the streets, I am in the hug you receive from a friend or parent, I am everywhere, in all things.

Life is hectic and it will overwhelm you if you don't take time every day to be still. Shut out the noise around you and listen to what is inside your heart, your soul. The spirit will guide you as you journey towards your center to find peace.

Find me my children, I am here, but you will find me quicker if you can just be still.

Be Brave

Be brave my children, stand strong in your faith and know that I am with you.

Fear is most often a tool of the enemy and it is used in many ways. It causes you to doubt yourselves and others, to panic and react, sometimes in a negative way. I do not use fear to teach my children, I teach you caution and to become aware so that you know what dangers are out there and how to avoid them.

Your spirit knows what is right and wrong. You must be brave and always choose what is right, even when it is not the popular choice,

When you see something wrong or someone in trouble you must be brave and stand up. When you hear people slander yourself or others, you must be brave and speak out. If you find yourself surrounded by fear and darkness you must be brave and shine. You have the strength of my spirit within you children, use it when you need to be brave.

There are many ecological and environmental problems in the world right now. I gave you a beautiful place to live but it is up to you to tend to it and take care of it. There are brilliant minds among you, that can get together and fix the problems but the collective must stand and be brave to stand up against those who do not care and ask the others to unite.

Man-made diseases run rampant throughout your lands and these are growing in occurrences. You must question where, why and how these are happening and not sit back in fear.

I have provided every type of plant that can heal and yet wellness is not being provided for the least of my children. They are no less worthy than another. Stand and be brave and work to get equality throughout the lands.

I know you get weary my children, but remember you are not alone. You are my children and I love you. When others persecute you for believing in me be brave. Stand strong in your faith and know that I await you and love you.

Whatever hardships you might face today my children, remember that I am with you and be brave

Lend A Helping Hand

Help each other my children. I gave you one another so you would have someone to love, someone you could support and who also would help you when times are tough.

You are not alone my children, I am with you and you have each other. When you see someone in need you must help them. When you see someone being hurt you must try and save them, and when you see someone in pain you must give them comfort.

Send your light out into the world so that others may be comforted by it. Help them out of their darkness and back into the light. I am with you and will give you strength as you go. You have my Spirit within you and it will provide what is needed.

When someone has nothing or very little you must share what you have with them. This way you will both be filled; no one needs to go without. There is abundance in the world … no one should be without when so many have so much. Share what you have with each other my children. Feed the hungry, clothe my children and teach them what you know for they are your brothers and your sisters.

If someone stumbles and falls give them your hand and help them up. I mean this literally and figuratively. When you need someone to support you and lift you up, they will be there and even if they are not my child know I am with you and carrying you.

Your hands are made for many things but one of the most precious ways to use them my children is to lend a helping hand.

You Are The Church

Do not forget my children that you have my Spirit in you and because of that you are also the church. The doors may be closed but your heart is open and your soul knows this.

While there are things you may not do, you always can study my word. Technology allows you to observe mass even when you cannot be present yourself. Read your bibles, say the rosary, talk to me, I am here.

Use the tools at your disposal my children so you can talk to each other. Pray together, even if it is over the phone or internet. These things are possible. The buildings will come and go but it is the gathering of people that allows me to be present. For now, a virtual gathering will suffice dear ones. When the time comes you can return to the buildings.

Please never forget that when you carry me within your heart you also carry the church. Your acts of kindness, compassion and love bring me to the world through you.

Be strong my children, when times are tough people need to hear from you. Be my voice and when you do that people will see that you are the church.

Be Thankful

Be thankful my children. I know in these dark times it is hard but you must not lose sight of all the things you have to be thankful for.

I have sent many angels to assist you my children; both heavenly and earthly angels descend to fight the battle of darkness. Give thanks for these angels children, even if you do not see them.

Those of you who have shelter, be thankful and try to help those of you that do not. These are the lesser of my children; the poor, the lost, the inflicted are all children of God. Find a way to help them through these dark times. I am with you and will give you strength.

To those of you who have food, find ways to share with those that do not. For them the struggle is harder than ever before and they need you, they will be ever thankful for you and your kindness and I will always remember what you did for my children in their time of need. Do not take more than you need, depriving others as you go, this too I see. There is enough if you all work together wisely.

For all those that are making it possible for you to continue to live, eat and be safe, you must give thanks. Without them it would be even darker and you'd be struggling more than you can ever imagine. Let them know you see them and make sure they know how thankful you are. Sing out, ring out and shout with thanks from where you shelter, they will hear you; you will bring light to the world with your love, compassion, kindness and thanksgiving.

I know you are struggling, don't lose hope, don't lose faith. I am with you and my angels are there. In your sorrows and your struggling never forget my children to still find ways to be thankful.

Keep Going

Keep going my children, do not lose hope. This too will pass.

I know you are struggling children, I've heard your prayers. I am listening, and I am with you in your sorrow and your time of struggle. I am with you in your isolation. I am here and I am working for you but everyone is not doing their part my precious ones.

There are people not listening, straying, and putting everyone at risk. As in the days of long ago, you must take shelter in your houses for this deathly virus to pass you by. You must not venture out into the storm or you risk bringing the storm to you and those you cherish.

I have welcomed home way more children than I should have had to. My house is open and all who enter are welcome and will be in a place of love and eternal joy, free from pain and suffering, but, this does not have to be. Do not dance on the edge, do not take the risks, I want you to live a full and happy life my children.

I am here when you all come home but you do not have to come yet. Stay inside and you will be passed over. Stay inside and protect your loved ones. Stay in touch using your technology.

Be smart and don't put my servants who are working vigilantly on the front line of this battle in extra harm. These are helpers I have put on earth for you. Don't take them for granted, don't put them at extra risk or there won't be enough of them to support you. You call them essential workers, I call them your earthly angels. Make sure they are looked after and kept safe so no harm comes to them or their family.

Never lose faith my children. This is a battle for which we all have our part. Yours is to stay inside so you can keep going.

You Are Forgiven

You are forgiven my children, remember that, not just at Easter, but always.

I have made the greatest sacrifice for you my children, please never forget. I sent you my heart, my son, so that he may bear the sin of the world and allow you to rejoin us when it is your time to come home. He led the way so that you could follow. Live by his example.

Follow my example children, forgive others as I have forgiven you. Forgive yourself, as I have forgiven you. When you do this you walk with, and in, my light.

Every day, take time to remember what has been given for you, so that you may return home. Every day remember me, remember the ultimate sacrifice paid for you and all who follow after you.

The gift my son gave to you is everlasting, meant not just for the people of His time but for all people throughout the ages who remember and believe. This is my gift to you my children, my sons' gift to you; cherish His gift of unfailing love,

He bore the pain so that you might live my children, please never forget what He has given you. Live a life that honours His gift. Forgive others and never forget that you are forgiven.

You Are Important

You are important to me my children. I love you more than you could know.

Please take care of yourself my children, I love you and want you to be well. Well in health and well in Spirit. You must do what is asked of you if you are to make it through. I have ensured you know what you need to do in order to survive your current turmoil.

Watch over each other, if even from a distance. Ask if someone has a need and try to help if you can. You can still help and be safe at the same time.

There is no lesser or greater among you. I love you all, sinner and saint alike. I will always love you, in this you can trust. There is no end to my infinite love, children.

Feel my love, my children. Spend time with me and you will feel it. Find the quiet space in each day; open your hearts to me. I am with you always, always waiting, just to spend time with you because you are important to me; you are a child of God.

When you are afraid, feeling lonely, lost or confused, draw on the strength of my love. I stand beside you, around you and my Spirit resides within you; an eternal love, meant for the children of God.

Never discount your strength, your courage, your heart. Never wonder if I love you, I do, because you, my child are important.

You Were Made To Shine

You were made to shine, my children. Do not withhold your light from the world.

You have my light, my Spirit, within you. I gave you my light so that you could shine and be a light to others in their time of need.

Everyone needs a light in their darkest hour. When you withdraw or withhold your light from someone, you subject them to pain, anger, self-hatred and isolation.

At some point you will need someone else to shine their light for you. Imagine now, if they refused, if they did not share their light by showing they cared, and then think about how that would make you feel.

Like the sunrise bringing the world out of darkness, you too can bring hope to a person by shining your light on them. Giving of yourself when another is in need is the greatest gift you can give; a gift of love is a gift of light.

A simple phone call to check on someone could lift them out of the depths of despair. You have that power, that gift, that light within you my children, do not be afraid to use it.

You are the beacon, the light in someone's storm. If you live by light, you may never even know you helped someone, that is truly a gift; unselfishly given unto the world, a light shone.

Never forget the power of love and light, after all my children, you were made to shine.

Be Careful

Be careful my children, the enemy is everywhere but fear not for I am with you.

I am here for you my children, do not turn away. The enemy has many servants trying to pull you away from me, to get you to turn your backs and stray. Do not be tempted, no matter how easy, fun or enticing it might seem.

If you do stray and wish to come back, I will be here, waiting. If you ask it of me sincerely, I will forgive you. This is the gift to you from my Son, the gift of forgiveness so that you can join me when your time comes. This gift however is not a free pass to go do whatever you want without consequence.

You must keep a watchful eye and a peaceful heart so that you are not pulled into the depths of despair, especially now during this trying time.

Despair and hopelessness are tools of the enemy; tools meant to separate you from love, and happiness, and me.

I am watching over you always, my children, but so is he. He is always waiting for an opening, an opportunity to pull you down towards him. Do not be fooled by his trickery.

Pray, talk with me, love one another and live a peaceful life. Be kind and compassionate but also be observant and alert. Never forget that I am with you my children.

Take me with you, in your heart and soul, wherever you go. Never forget that when you go out into the world you need to be aware of your surroundings. Be watchful, be mindful and be careful.

Be At Peace

Be at peace my children, the storm is almost over.

I see the struggle you are having and how hard you are trying. I hear your prayers children, and want you to know that your struggle is not in vain. The time is coming when you can rest easy, knowing that you have completed the task asked of you.

There is hope in your belief, and therefore no situation is ever hopeless. I see your faith in me, and with faith comes peace; the peace of knowing all is never lost forever. I am with you, I hear you, and you are never alone.

This word peace has been used in many ways and has a few different meanings, but to the faithful it means tranquility; for no war can rage when there is peace, no evil prevails when the enemy rejected.

Everyone wants to feel at ease, at peace within. These days children, I can see how hard at times that has been for you. Do not fret, for I am with you and my Spirit resides within you. Draw upon the Spirit and you will know peace. Live a life of love and you will know peace.

My peace I grant to you children. If you live in love truly, then you desire peace for not only yourself and your family, but for all. My peace is meant for everyone, and everyone who seeks me shall find it.

Do not lose faith children, the time is coming when the things that trouble you disappear. Until that time comes, know that I am with you and be at peace.

You Have What It Takes

You have what it takes children, do not doubt it, or fear, for I am with you always.

I have given you all you need, my children, to succeed, to be happy and to be safe. You just have to look around and you will see it.

Somethings you must work for, because it is in working that you find self-worth. It is in working that you are able to provide the basic necessities for yourself and your family. You have what it takes to fulfill this task,

Somethings I have given for your senses, to make you smile and feel joy. The sun and stars shining, the beautiful flowers, so much in nature provided just for you. Family and friends who love you, who make you want to love in return.

Love is the greatest gift and the greatest request; love one another as you love yourself. Perhaps at times love another even more than you love yourself, but love none the less.

Love is what will bring peace to your world. You have all the love you need to make your life peaceful and meaningful.

I have sent angels to walk among you and to watch over you. They help you when you don't even know it, but they are there all the same. It doesn't matter if you see or know them. That is not their goal, their goal is to guide, and keep you safe.

Some of my angels keep you safe from things you cannot even see, evils that exist in the darkness. These are my warriors sent for you.

When you are afraid remember you are not alone and you have what you need to survive and keep going.

You have all that you need. You have what it takes to live a good, honest life. A life full of kindness, compassion and love my child.

Each one of you has a talent and that talent will help you fulfill your purpose. Do not doubt yourself, my children for you have what you need inside you; you have what it takes.

Find Hope In Me

Find hope in me, my children, all is not lost. I am with you always and that in itself is a message to bring you hope.

When life gets you down, or is frightening, you can call on me. I am with you always, watching, listening, and loving you. This will never change. You are my beloved children, today, tomorrow, forever.

When you think there is nowhere left to turn, turn to me. I am always here and ever listening. There is nothing so bad that can't be forgiven my child. If you ask it of me with an honest and sincere heart, I will hear you and you will be forgiven. That is the gift my Son gave to you, I gave to you and with it brings eternal hope.

The sorrows of this world are not forever. Your time here may feel long but it is fleeting in comparison to an eternity with me. Do not despair, do not give in to darkness; shine your light for all the world to see and you will never be lost.

While each of you are uniquely made, you are of me and therefore you have the inner strength to endure anything that is thrown at you; no evil can exist in this light of the mine.

Even if you turn and walk away from me, I will not forget you my children. I will be here waiting for your return. I will not turn away from you ever; my sights are set upon my children always.

Things can change, get better, as long as you take steps and do not dwell in the darkness. It is in the darkness that hope seems lost, but not for you, never for you, my child.

You have my light within you. When the darkness comes, look inside and find the light. Feed the flame within you until it surrounds you, expanding beyond yourself to others.

There is a peace that comes with prayer. An open, honest heart, reaching out to me. When all seems lost my children, do not despair, find hope in me.

You Are Disciples

You are my disciples children. Lead the way for others, show them your light and they will see mine. Show them your love and they will know me through you.

When you teach your children about me, you are my disciples. As your children grow in faith they too become disciples, showing the way for others.

When you share my messages with others you are my disciple. People will hear you but also watch you. Live a life of goodness and love, helping those in need. My children will follow suit; they will live a life true to their Spirit.

Hate is bred by ignorance and darkness, you children, must be a light to the world; my light entrusted to you.

When you live a life obeying the commandments I have left, you set the example and are thus my disciples. You show others that it is possible to live an honest, wholesome and happy life. A life filled with love and understanding, filled with compassion and kindness. These are my ways children, and when you live them you become my disciples.

You do not need to perform miracles to be a disciple of mine, but know it is within your power when you believe and live by the light of the Spirit given into you.

Each of you has it within you to light the way for all who cross your path. Never forget this children, never forget that you are disciples.

I Hear You

I hear you my children and I am here. Do not give up hope for I am with you always.

These are troubling times my children, do not lose faith for I am with you. I hear your cries, your prayers and I know your hearts. Only in standing up for what is right and good will things change.

My children must band together now, closer than ever. The enemy has many puppets in the world right now. If you live by the light you will be able to recognize them. Your light casts shadows on the darkness, revealing the truth. Shine your light bright and together you can overcome the darkness. Good always wins over evil; no darkness prevails in the light, no hatred in love.

Surround yourself with my light, my love. It is a protection for you; a guide that will eventually bring you home to me. That time is not yet my children but there will be a day when you are called home and I will be here waiting to greet you.

My angels are fighting hard for you. They come in many forms to cast out evil, to protect you and aid you in your time of need. If you look hard enough, you will see them, their numbers are growing.

Continue to raise your voices, continue to pray and know that always I am here, and I hear you.

Walk And Talk Awhile With Me

I walk with you always children even when you don't see me. Will you walk and talk awhile with me?

I am there by your side, listening and walking right alongside you. It doesn't matter where you go, I will walk with you. I am your constant companion, someone who listens to you, and who loves you as you journey through life. You just need to open your heart and listen with your Spirit to know what I say is true.

I go with you wherever you go. Even when you don't always want to walk with me. At times you are pulled off the path of light; yet still I walk with my children so they can be guided home.

As you walk along your path of life, I am there children, often asking if you'll walk and talk awhile with me. Your answer changes back and forth over the years, needing me when things are difficult and forgetting about me at times when things are good. It doesn't matter how hard or easy your journey is children, I will be there for you always.

When you get anxious, go outside and take a walk with me. You don't have to speak out loud for me to hear you, your thoughts are heard. We can have wonderful talks to ease your anxiousness. If walking is difficult, that is okay too, as you can visualize us walking.

I hear you no matter where you are or what you are doing. If you would prefer, you can sit awhile, kneel awhile, play awhile and talk with me as you do.

Many of my children are lost and have turned from me. They need you also. When the opportunity presents itself please sit and talk with them awhile. I will be there with you.

I will come and walk with you in your day, whenever and wherever you want me to. The question children is this, will you walk and talk awhile with me?

You Know How To Find Me

You know how to find me children, I am right there standing at your side. I am of the earth, the wind and sky. Seek and you shall find.

In your time of need, search inside and you will know how to find me. You are linked to me children, through the Holy Spirit and therefore can find me at any moment in time. Use the link between us to reach out and find me.

The Spirit will not only guide you, it will help protect you, but you must invoke it. By this, I mean you must call upon your Spirit to surround you in a loving protection of light, my protection. You must ask the Spirit to guide you in your journey, to help guide you to me.

Wherever you go, I am there. You can talk to me and I will hear. I always answer you my children. I answer in many different ways so you need to be alert, listen and watch. You may not always understand my answer but there is a reason for everything and one day I promise you will understand.

When you go to church, I am there. I am present and with you at the mass. You are with me as I am with you; never shall you be alone when you are in the house of the Lord.

I am the homeless person you pass on the street. I am the beggar and the cripple. I am the elderly neighbour in need of your assistance. I am all people who cross your path and need assistance. When you help them, you help me.

Come to me in prayer and you will find me. You can pray at anytime, anywhere and I will not only hear you, I will be there. In your sorrow, in your joy, I am there.

Search your heart and let your Spirit guide you. If you look inside you will realize that you have all you need. You know how to find me.

I Am Here

You are not forgotten children, I am here.

I am all around you, lifting you up, giving you hope. All you need to do is look and you will see that I am right here, beside you, always.

I could not, and will not, forget you, or leave you, ever. You are my child and I will remain with you. I send you signs of my presence every day.

I am in the rising and setting of the sun, moon and stars. I am in the gentle breeze, the rain and the air that you breathe. I am all around you, look for me, I am here.

You are my children, carved from my love. You are a part of me. I could not leave you even if I wanted because you are in me and I am in you; engrained and entwined is my love, we are one throughout eternity.

When you talk and pray to me, I am here. When you cry out in pain, sorrow and suffering, I am here. Even when you believe you are alone, you are not, for I am here, always here, by your side.

I send angels of all kinds as a sign of my presence. I send messages through the people you interact with and in the music that you listen to. Be aware though that the enemy also does this. You must listen and watch with your spirit so you can see me. When you do this, you will know in the very depths of your heart and soul that I am present.

I know there are times when things are difficult for you. I am not testing you, I am here, helping you get through it. Draw on me for your strength; lean on me and I shall help you in your journey.

Never doubt that I am here, never question if I love you. I am and I do, always. Nothing you can do will push me away. If you turn from me, I will still be here waiting. Your eyes, though veiled, can find me again when you turn back in my direction. I will not leave, I will remain here.

If you are feeling lost or forgotten child, have no fear, for I am by your side. Never forget my love for you, never forget that always I am here.

Stay In The Light

Stay in the light my children, keep away from the darkness of the enemy.

There is a darkness brewing children, trying to tempt you and pull you away from me. You must stand strong and stay in the light. You have all the strength you need to resist temptation for I am with you.

I am saddened when any of my children leave and walk towards the darkness. I can feel their struggle, their sadness, their doubt and sometimes their anger. The enemy feeds off of these, luring and enticing them with lies and trickery. I will be here waiting for them to step back into the light but the choice is theirs alone. I will continue to shine my light and send angels their way to assist them.

Surround yourself with my light my children so that you can shine bright. You were meant to shine, meant to be a guide for others. You are meant to love and be loved, to live in the light and shine it outwards; a beacon, helping others come home safely from the dark storm.

The light will warm you and embrace you. If you call upon it, the light will protect you, keeping you safe. You can place a circle of protection around you and the ones you love. This will help shield them from the darkness of the enemy. You have my Spirit, it is strong, embrace it, use it.

When you live in the light you are of me, living flesh, that represents all that
is good. It is on this same light that you will journey home when the time comes. Home, where there is light and life everlasting.

Be warned, the darkness of the enemy is everywhere. It is violent and vulgar, obscene and uncaring. It hides in many forms and in many places. There are servants of the darkness all around the world, trying to increase their numbers. They are disguised as leaders, entertainers and sometimes false friends. You will recognize them if you stay in the light and look at them with eyes of love. Whenever confronted, the enemy will shrink from light and love.

You have everything you need to shine. I have shown you the way children, all you need to do is to stay in the light.

Bring Me With You

Bring me with you my children, in all that you do and I will be with you always. In your waking and in your slumber bring me with you. In your going out or staying in, bring me with you. In your time of need or time of joy bring me with you.

I want to be with you children, in everything you do. When you start your day, if you ask it of me, I will journey with you. You can make me present by the way you walk throughout your day. Be kind, generous, compassionate and loving. When you live this way, you carry me out into the world.

I am your greatest armour. Surround yourself with my white and loving light, ask for it to be a shield of protection. It will keep your Spirit safe from all darkness but you must ask for it, you must carry it, which means children, you must bring me with you.

I walk alongside of you always, but in order for you to fully bring me with you throughout your days you must commune with me children. You must ask, in prayer, openly and honestly.

My people recognize me in others by the way they live. I come across in their actions, their words and their love. You can see me in their faces as they shine, even in the sad and hard times, they carry me with them. I am in their tears and in their smiles, their hope and in their fears.

Bring me with you in your work, always giving your best. Treat others the way you would be treated, the way I have treated you. Be kind and patient. Do not grow angry if they do not meet your expectations, perhaps they did not know fully what you expected. Tell them gently, show them how, and be involved. Get to know your peers and leaders and let them know you.

Bring me into your relationships, your marriages. When you pray together I will be with you. Always act towards each other with love. Be open and honest with each other, even when it is difficult. Lean on each other when times are hard. Support each other, always lifting each other up. Be faithful to one another. When you do these things, you bring me into your relationships and I am with you.

When you raise your children, bring me into their lives. Teach them about me. Show them how to pray and carry me with them throughout their day. Raise them to be honest, kind people. Let them know it is okay to fail, tell them it is not the failing that people will remember, it is how they rise from their failures. If they bring me with them they can rise and shine for all the world to see.

I want to be with you children in all that you do but in order for that to happen, you must bring me with you.

Lean On Me

Lean on me children, I am strong enough to carry you and your burdens.

When things are tough and you need strength, lean on me children. I will help you get through the rough patches. You need to trust me to do it. You will have the courage and strength that you need. You've already endured much and you are still here.

During times of sadness, I am with you. You can look to me and find comfort. I hold your loved ones in my arms, and will hold you when your time comes. My light wraps around you always to comfort you, draw strength from it. When you lean on me, things are not as overwhelming, but you must believe and trust that I am there helping you.

When you are lonely, I am there. Lean on me for companionship and understand that you are never alone. I am by your side, loving you, always. Close your eyes and take a deep breath, you will find me in the silence. Even amongst the busiest of gatherings you can find me. You are never alone.

When you are tired and need rest, lean on me. Rest and be at peace knowing that I am watching over you. I will keep you safe my children. You are my light, and that light is protected by me always. Use it, follow it, and draw from it. It will give you the energy to continue when times are bad, and replenish you when your well runs dry.

I will never abandon you, hurt you or walk away from you. When you need me, I am there. You are my children and I love you. If you need help, I am there. Know children, and believe, that you can always lean on me.

Replenish Yourselves

Replenish yourselves my children, do not let your wells run dry.

It is important that you look after yourselves children. You need to take care of yourself physically, mentally and spiritually. Please do not drain yourself to the point of being completely empty or you will be unable to function. You will become exhausted and unable to do the works required of you.

Even now, when many are still shut inside, I see you are being drained. You are not taking care of yourself. I need you my children. Take care of yourselves. I need you to be able to help others. You cannot do this if you lose sight of yourself.

Eat at my table, drink from my cup and I will restore you. I know this is hard for you to do right now. Many gathering places for worship are closed, or hard to get into as space has been limited. I am still here though, offering myself to you. If you allow me to, I can still flow in, and through you. In this way I can replenish you, until you can physically eat again at my table.

With my light, you can gather strength, but you must do your part. Pray, ask for my light to surround you, and flow through you, and to protect you and your loved ones. Ask and believe children, and it will be done.

Make sure you are getting the proper nourishment. You must eat healthily to maintain your fitness level. Remain in good shape so that you are able to sustain the life I need of you. In order for you to be able to help others, you must take care of yourselves physically. Even a shepherd must rest at times while tending his flock.

Keep your mind active children. Do not fill it with violence and filth. Stimulate it, expand it, exercise it. In this way you stay alert and healthy. In this way you can avoid depression and sadness.

You are my beloved children. I do not want to see you lacking. I do not want to see you run yourselves ragged and dry until you are an empty vessel. I need you my children. I love you. Please look after one another. Please don't forget to replenish yourselves.

You Are Not Alone

You are not alone, my children, I am with you.

I am always with you, supporting you, shielding you, loving you. You are as much a part of me as I am of you; carved in my hand, never to be forgotten.

You are never alone when you carry me with you. Draw strength from me, my children. When you know, and trust that I am there you can draw on me for your courage.

I also have sent you angels, to watch over you and assist you in your time of need. You may not always see them but they are there. They come in many forms throughout your life, easing your pain and suffering, soothing your sorrow.

Even when you turn away from me, I am there. These are the darkest times for you and I could never leave your side. Though you turn towards the darkness, my light is there waiting, always at your side, at your back, waiting. When you are ready to turn back you will find and see my light.

In your time of isolation and sickness, you are not alone. Though you walk a path by yourself, unsupported by others, you are not alone. When you are in despair, hurting, full of sorrow, you are not alone. I am there always and this will never change, my children.

You, after all are my children. Though a parent may forget or leave their child, I will not leave you, my children. You are engrained in me, woven into the very fabric of life itself. I am with you always.

Knowing I am there, find comfort in me when you begin to struggle. Pray and talk to me. Find gratitude and joy in my presence. Feel the light I have shone towards you and through you. Let its' love embrace you, and then share it with others so they too may know they are not alone.

Do not despair my children for I am with you always. I love you children. Always remember that you are not alone.

I Love You

I love you my children, I would never abandon you. Do not give up hope for I am with you. I am there with you children, watching everything you do. Always I am by your side, encouraging you, sending you signs. I am your biggest fan.

You are of me, a part of me, my children. I could never forget you or abandon you. Please do not blame me for the works of the enemy.

My angels are fighting against him continually, but he grows stronger based on the choices my children have been making. He knows he cannot win, but he will create as much damage and chaos as he can in the meantime.

If you look close enough, you can see me, in many ways. I can be found in the works of others. You can see me in the beauty of all living things.

I can be found even in those who are in the direst of circumstances. If you look closely you will see me. I am in the stranger putting their own life at risk to save another, in the laughter of a child, in the words of a song sent to you just at the right time. I am in the essence of the wind, the swaying of the trees and the rising and setting of the sun.

Please stop trying to test my love for you my children, just to see if I am real. I will never stop loving you. Too many of my children only believe in me, if I pull them out of a bad circumstance, one that their own choices have put them in. Even when I do, at times, they still doubt.

Nothing you can do will change my love for you. You may walk away, but I will still be here, loving you. If you turn back, I am here to receive you once again.

You have free will, to make your own choices. Understand this though, belief in me cannot be conditional, my children. When you open your heart to receive me, I will fill it abundantly. When you turn to me, you must leave the enemy behind.

I know your heart, and your struggles. You are not perfect, my children, but you have the capacity to do wonderful things. Acts of love and kindness help build and strengthen your spirit, showing my love for the world through you.

Like a child you are still learning. Do not denounce the things I put in front of you, at times for your own safety, in my name. Do not belittle, maim or kill others, in my name. That is not love, you were made from love, to love. Each with a purpose, each with a talent.

My messages have been twisted across the years, but this one is true and will never change, I love you, my children.

Do Not Walk With The Wicked

Do not walk with the wicked, my children, it will turn you away from my light and toward the darkness.

When you use my light children, you can see the path in front of you. It is when you turn away that the road becomes dark, and you will find yourself stumbling. You will not be able to see the traps set out in front of you, no matter how obvious they are.

I have given you a conscience my children, to know what is right and true from what is wrong and hurtful. Use it to guide you. Let it show you the path to walk. Listen to it and it will guide you. It is my link to you, my Spirit, ever guiding.

When you hang around people who are mean spirited, vulgar and immoral for any length of time, you begin to take on their cloak. You become shielded from the light until you only see darkness. This is what the enemy wants, to turn you away from the light, towards the darkness.

You can see the darkness all around the world. It is found in those who hurt others, who steal and who think only of themselves. You will find it in those who say hateful things, belittle and bully others for their own enjoyment. It can be found in the ones causing havoc during a peaceful protest. They destroy property, steal, aim to hurt others. Their actions are not based out of love, or doing what is right. The actions of those in darkness are based out of rage and hatred.

People of darkness try to hide in plain sight. Sometimes so much so that others begin to believe their ways are normal and just. However, if you look inside to your compass, your conscience, you will know right from wrong; it is like ill-fitting clothes that hang from your body, causing you to trip and fall.

Surround yourself with children of the light. They truly stand for what is right, living lives based in love. Children of the light are kind, compassionate and loving, even when the world has thrown them one curve after another. These people are helping those in need and are well intentioned. You can see their light as they let it shine for all the world to see.

Some of my children have been lost to me, but there are so many walking in the light still. Walk with the those of the light my children, do not walk with the wicked.

Be Not Troubled

Be not troubled my children for I am with you always. You can weather any storm life throws your way.

I am always with you children, helping you. Trust that I will never leave you. You are never alone nor far from me. Though at times, events can be disturbing do not carry the disturbance in your heart. You can acknowledge it without owning it.

I know that you are afraid at times, but know that I have given you what you need to get through anything that comes your way. There are signs, given for you, so that you will know which way to go, and where to turn in your times of trouble.

Do not let the burdens or concerns of others weigh you down. Though you may help them, you do not need to wear their worries on your sleeve. You can be a comfort and a friend to one in need always. Let your light shine to help them through.

Likewise, people will be there for you. I have angels everywhere helping in your time of need. My angels come in many forms. Some, you may not ever see or be aware of their presence. Know that they are there helping you and protecting you.

The world is currently in a turbulent state, children. Make a positive change, knowing you can help turn things around in all impacted areas.

Do not turn a blind eye when you see someone struggling, or something that is wrong occurring around you. Also, do not be overwhelmed or troubled.

You are not alone, ever. I am with you always and you can call on me. I will always answer you, though at times you may not understand the answer. Faith, is having trust in me, even when you can't see what is ahead for you.

Never forget that I am with you my children. When times are hard, remember that you can get through it. Life on this earth is short, so spend it wisely, and be not troubled.

Choose Your Words Carefully

Choose your words carefully my children, they can soothe but they can also torment.

Words are powerful children. Be careful of the words you use when talking to yourself, your spouse, your children, your friends and all others. You can do great things with words but you can also bring great harm.

You were meant to love and be loved. With this in mind you should use words that encourage and uplift. Always use words that soothe and bring comfort to another who is hurting. Use them to teach and to praise others.

Do not use words to put down another, or to be hurtful. Even if someone has wronged or hurt you, do not try to hurt them back. This is when you use words of forgiveness. Forgive them their ignorance and uneducated ways. An educated person is knowledgeable and understands that you are all my children, and as such, are to be loved without condition.

Your words carry weight so do not use them to humiliate, discourage, antagonize or encourage violence and hatred. This is not what you were made for. There are too many people today, too many of my children, who have forgotten this.

They slander, swear, and use words to fan the flames of disrespect and hatred. Do not be like them children, be better.

Also, do not use negative, hurtful and harmful words on yourself. You are my child, beautiful in all your glory. Do not belittle or put yourself down. Yes, you can always do better, be better; you are love embodied in flesh, treat yourself as such.

Negative, harmful words lead to anger, self-isolation and sadness. All lead you off your intended path and diminish your light. Make a choice every day to only use words of encouragement, praise and love. If all my children did this, there would be no wars, no hatred, no violence.

Always remember that your words reflect who you are to the world children. Be a reflection of my love and choose your words carefully.

Open Your Hearts to Love

Open your hearts to love my children. You were made to love and to be loved.

Do not fear love children. It is a joyful gift and one of my greatest commandments; love one another as I have loved you. Do not be afraid to open up your hearts for you have a great capacity to love.

Your hearts know no limits and can love more than you are even aware. Love everyone you meet. There is no one you cannot love if you look at them through my eyes.

Even your enemies can be loved. When you love your enemies, you see them with eyes of sorrow instead of eyes of hatred. They are my lost souls who need your love more than anyone else. When you shine the light of my love on them they become changed. Some will shy away from the light and will take longer than others to see and feel the effects of your light, your love. Know that they will feel it and will be forever changed because of it.

Everyone can be changed with love. When you love you are more joyful and your Spirit is at peace. If, however, you refuse to love, protecting your heart to avoid being hurt, then you are cheating yourself and all those around you.

Yes, love comes at a cost sometimes. You will lose someone you love, but if you have faith and believe in me, you will know that no one is lost to you. All will be reunited in my kingdom. A place where all sorrow and pain exist no more. A place where you only know love and joy.

There is always a risk that when you love, you will not be shown love in return … love anyway. When you love someone and show them kindness, they see me through you. They find me; for those that love are of me, and those that are of me love.

When you close your heart off to love you will eventually become bitter, often angry. Life is a lonely place without love. You children, are all brothers and sisters and as such are family … love one another as I love you.

Never shut the door on love for when you do this you are shutting the door on me my children.

Do not be afraid children, open your hearts to love.

Have Courage

Have courage my children, for I am with you. If you believe in me do not fear; for your heart and longings are known to me.

My angels are surrounding you, fighting an unseen battle this very moment. The times are getting worse and they are needed more than ever. They will come to you if you call them. My angels will protect you, they have the strength of thousands but you are also strong.

You have the strength you need within you. I have given you strength to fight the enemy, to endure loss and sadness and to change the world for the better. You, my children, have the power to tip the scales away from darkness and back towards the light.

There are many signs being given to you, many opportunities in front of you. Opportunities to make things better, spend more time with those that matter and help those who need it.

You are stronger than you give yourself credit for and you are capable of much. Do not discount your worth my children for you have unique talents. Talents, given by me, to you. Share them with the world.

When you begin to fear, call on me and stand strong. Straighten your back and meet the challenges in front of you. If you do not think you are capable, remember that you are. Nothing is impossible when you believe and have faith.

Your will and faith will be tested these coming days, not by me, but by the enemy. The enemy is always testing, looking for a weakness, an opportunity to turn you away from me and towards him. Remember this and do not falter. When these times are upon you have courage and stand strong.

Shine your light brightly out into the world. When you do this, you will attract others, drawing their light to yours. Together you can dispel the darkness, not with violence but with acts of love, kindness and compassion. These are your strengths, the things that illuminate your light and feed the Spirit.

The Spirit is your very essence, the source of your light, my light. The darkness cannot exist in this light.

Yes, my children these are trying times. I cannot promise they will get better right away. Remember always that you are not alone. My angels are fighting, right this second and every moment that follows. They are fighting for you, for the entire world.

Stand strong in your faith my children. Remember who you are. You are a child of the God, housing my Spirit. Never forget the gift my Son gave you, and have courage.

Do Not Become Complacent

Do not become complacent my children, indifference opens the door for the enemy.

Be aware, do not become complacent or indifferent to the gifts you have been given. These are gifts for you to share with the world so that all can become better, be at peace and find joy. Your talents are for others, not for your own self-satisfaction. While you can take momentary joy in your achievements, don't rest there for long. Continue using and sharing your gifts with the world.

There is a complacency throughout the world right now which should not exist. Violence, vulgarity, thievery and immoral acts are being performed, aided by the enemy, daily. I am saddened because my children should be shocked and appalled by this but they seem to sit back and barely blink anymore.

All around the world social media, television and radio spurt untruths and ask you to choose. They ask you, children, to choose the ways of loose morals, corrupt thinking and work to pull you away from the truth of the Spirit. Do not buy into the thinking that money is better than Spirit and material things will bring you more joy than anything else.

Every day peoples' self-esteem is spiralling downward because they have bought into the concept that they are not good enough, thin enough, worth enough. You are my children, and you are perfectly made. Hold fast to your true self, your authentic being. Stay in tune with the Spirit given unto you.

Until my children step forward, say 'enough', stop buying into untruths, watching violence and vulgarity, and speak out against all abhorrent behaviour, things will continue to get worse. The enemy will dance with glee at the laziness and indifference of my children.

You must be strong and stand up for yourself, your family and all the children that follow in your line. Stand for your neighbours, for your friends and for strangers when you see them being treated unfairly or abusively. Show others the way. Stand for truth, justice and light.

You must speak out, rejecting violence and vulgarity, obscenity and unlawful behaviour. You, my children, must always stand for what is right. Live in the light and hold fast to your faith in me. I will never leave you or abandon you. Truly I tell you, all who believe in me and live according to my will shall be welcomed in my kingdom.

Times are growing increasingly dangerous children, the path to me is clear. Be strong, have faith, be aware and on alert and whatever you do, do not become complacent.

Do Not Hate

Do not hate in my name children. Be at peace with one another. Love one another.

If one of my sheep is lost, help it find its' way home. You are here to be a guide for all, those in my flock, and those who are lost. Guide them with love and compassion.

Those who are lost cannot see my light if you are yelling, or carrying out acts of hatred in my name. These acts broadcast only darkness and not light. In these troubling times all my children must shine brighter.

My message is always one of love. True love does not hate, it does not judge, it only loves. Love one another. See each other through my eyes and you will not be capable of hate.

I did not make you better than the other, only different. Each with your own set of gifts, your own unique talents, that will allow you to uplift and shine. You are my children, love each other as such.

What is happening with my children in many parts of the world saddens me. I see anger and hatred, all turning into violence against one another. This is the work of my enemy, do not be his puppets children.

Be aware and alert. When you see anger brewing amongst the masses that is turning into hatred and violence, remove yourself. Be angry at the work of the enemy, do not accept his work but do not become a servant to it either. Hatred and violence only lead down his road and not mine.

Stand for justice children, but do it with love and light, dignity and grace, these are my ways. If they do not listen, walk away and uphold my values as you go. In this way they will see and know my light and my love.

There are many ways to show my light to the world through love children. Whatever you do make sure your anger does not turn you away from me. Do not hate.

Be Gentle With Each Other

Be gentle with each other children, you are all special to me.

You children are all my lambs, as such you are all in need of tending. In as much as you are a lamb, you are also a shepherd. You need to treat each other with kindness and compassion, with respect and love. You must watch out for each other. This is how my flock will flourish.

Do not speak harshly with one another. Speak only with words of love. If you cannot do this, be aware and remain silent. It is better to hold your tongue than to use it as a weapon. Do not spew hurtful words at each, be understanding and gentle with each other

When you see one of my children in need, you must try to help them, even if it is difficult. If my child is lost you must be my shepherd and find them, bringing them back into the flock where they can be safe and cared for.

Loving is not always easy children but it is the chosen path for you. I will provide you with the strength and endurance to survive the journey. I will even provide assistance when you need it. You are not alone, I have many children and therefore have many shepherds.

Recognize children that you are all still learning, each of you is at a different level. As such each of you requires help at one time or another. As you are there for others, so too will others be there for you.

Be not at war with one another, be at peace. Help each other to grow in love and faith. Build each other up, do not tear each other down. Do not hate, but love one another because of your differences, not your similarities. You are all the same inside, each having a great capacity for love.

Do not be harsh with another. Settle yourself and find calm within so that you can interact in a loving manner. Angry words do not nurture they only harm and hurt, leaving scars as they go.

If someone hurts you, do not retaliate, rather turn the other cheek. If you ask how many times,
I say to you as many are as needed. This doesn't mean putting yourself in a dangerous situation on purpose, it means forgiving. Some lost sheep require a different shepherd.

Hold hope in your hearts and carry faith with you as you journey. Never forget that I am with you. When you meet others on your journey remember that they too are my children.

Be kind children. Let your path be one of light and love as you journey. When you come across one another on life's' travels remember to be gentle with each.

Count Your Blessings

Count your blessings my children, for they are many.

Many gifts have been given unto you children, yet many are still taking them for granted. Some of you have forgotten what gifts you have and as a result are sad, depressed, lonely and occasionally bitter.

Though the world may be in turmoil and the enemy at work, I am still present. There are signs of my love everywhere. In the volunteers running into buildings to rescue others with little thought for themselves, or those sheltering the lost and forgotten children. Others, feeding and working with the poor and inflicted. So many of my children giving of themselves, daily, to help another. They are a blessing for the world and they are blessed in return.

You child, are alive. Your heart is beating and sustaining you. The physical one keeping you alive, the figurative one allowing you to love purely and freely.

So many of my children have less than you do, and yet, they are more grateful. They take pleasure in the simplest of things. The birds singing, the smell of leaves as they walk through a fall forest. There is beauty in the sunrise and the sunset. Beauty in the heavens where the clouds form and the stars shine.

Do not focus on what you do not have children, it will put you in a state of always wanting. Focus, rather on what you do have, on what you can give to the world. These are your blessings.

You woke up today, this is a blessing. As you are reading this, again you are blessed with sight and understanding. If you contemplate what you read, you are blessed with a functioning mind.

Some of you have shelter and food. This is more than others have. Share your blessings with others so they, in turn, can be blessed. Blessings are not to be found in material things, these do not last. Material blessings may make life easier, but no true blessing can be found if you do not share it with others.

Promise me children that you will not take your life for granted. Live with purpose. Be giving and loving, kind and compassionate. Let your Spirit shine for all the world to see.

Those who house a grateful heart can easily see their blessings. If you do not see, or know your blessings, set some time aside my children and contemplate. Never forget to count your blessings.

I Will Never Leave You

I will never leave you, my children. Know that I am here and always with you.

I know that many of you are feeling alone and forgotten. You are not alone. I am always with you, right by your side, housed within your Spirit. You can find me, in all my children, whose path you will cross daily.

This is true, you are of me, and as such, I cannot forget you. You, are as much a part of me, as I am of you. You may turn away from me, but my gaze will never turn from you. I will be with you always, watching, listening and providing assistance on your journey.

If you leave me, I will still be here, waiting for your return. I will send assistance your way, to help and to guide you. The choice to leave is always yours, this is free will. Just know, that you, my child, are woven into the fabric of life, my fabric.

I have assigned angels to all my children from the time of their conception. They will watch over you until you return home. These too are my gift to you. Use them. Call on them when you are in need. Thank them when they intervene and assist you. Talk to them. Get to know them. In doing so you are drawn closer to me as well.

Rather than blame me for the world's suffering, your suffering, figure out how you can help. What can you do? When you ease the suffering of those around you, I am there. I am the child suffering, alone, and in the lonely and forgotten.

Putting others before yourself is an act of love. In these acts you will find me. I am found in consideration and compassion, kindness and thoughtfulness. Living with these traits, you shine. When you shine, it is my light the world will see, allowing others to also know that I am here and have not left them.

Should you choose to walk away from the path of light, be warned. The path of darkness is that of the enemy. It is a path on which I do not exist. Know that it is a path of loneliness and anger, pain and frustration. This doesn't mean that I have left you, it means that I am here, on the path of light waiting for you to return.

I have sent angels into the darkness to help you. These angels will shine their light for you, so you, child, can find your way home. The paths are side by side. It only takes one step to return to the path of light. I am here, on the path of light, waiting. I am here always.

These continue to be trying times for all of my children. The enemy is pushing hard. Do not forget that he cannot win. Hold fast to your light and you will never lose hope.

Always remember and hold these words in your heart, I will never leave you, my children.

I Am Calling You

Listen, children can you hear me? I am calling you. Come to me, oh, my children.

I am calling out to you, heed my call. You are my sheep and I am calling you to safety. Hear my call. Come away from the hills of despair and sorrow. Come to my light. I am shining it for you; a beacon, navigating my children home.

Many of you are wandering away, lured by lies and deception. Do not let the ignorant educate you in their ways. They know not the truth, for they have been blinded. Lies have been passed down through the ages in a continual effort to coax you from me.

Close your eyes and open your heart to me. Let your Spirit guide you, my Spirit. When you do this, you will hear me. When you listen from the soul you will hear me calling you.

Many deny my Son, saying he was just a man, a prophet. He was both of these, yes, but he was also my Son. He was my gift to the world; a gift, given freely for my children. He was sent to show you the way, sent to make it possible for you to rejoin me. He has borne much for you, do not deny Him.

The tide is shifting and I am coming. When I do, I will raise my flock and bring them to eternal peace. Those who hear me know. The one who listens without talking hears, the one who talks without listening becomes lost.

Quiet your mind, shut it off to all things obscene and lurid. Object to violence, bigotry and vulgarity, there is no place for them in my world. Stand for truth, honesty, integrity and love. Recognize and reward integrity, compassion and kindness. These are traits of the light, of me, and of my Son.

When you are feeling lost and you cannot find your way, close your eyes and listen. Search inward. When you tune into your Spirit you will hear me, for I am calling you.

Be Like A Mustard Seed

Be like a mustard seed my children, strong in faith, generous with love.

Though the mighty seed may seem small and insignificant, in truth it is exceptional. From a small seed grows a big tree. A tree, that when nurtured, provides sustenance. This is a seed, that when fully developed, provides something that enhances other food.

So too can you grow in love and kindness. Grow, in fact so big that you can evolve further than you know. Though you are just one among millions you can reach across the earth, touching many as you go.

A strong faith shines a great light. It knows that there is always hope and that nobody can take you away from your ultimate destination. Share that faith with others so they too can grow, just like the mustard seed.

Enrich the lives of others. Shine the light of my love on them. Treat them with compassion, kindness and understanding. Accept my children for who they are and love them, wholly and fully.

A seed remains just a seed if it is not planted. Your love cannot flourish if it is not shared. Your faith cannot grow if it is not expressed. Do not remain stagnant nor turn a blind eye to the problems of this world. Also, do not shrivel like an unplanted seed.

The mustard seed is hardy and resilient, growing often in difficult soil. It is known to move rocks out of its path as it grows into a tree. Be resilient children, remove obstacles in your path.

There are many examples in nature for you, all of them different. Some are examples of what to do, others what not to do. This one though provides great awareness and wisdom if you are open to the lesson.

Oh, my children, hear what I am telling you, be like a tiny mustard seed.

Find Refuge In Me

When you are scared, lonely or hurt find refuge in me, my children.

Life can be hard at times but you can find peace within me. Even when at times you do not understand, I am here for you. I am always by your side, loving and embracing you. I will never you.

In me, you can find rest when times are troubling. Pass your worry over and I will carry it for you. Understand, however, that if you take it back I will give it to you.

I understand it is hard at times for you to stop worrying. There is a plan greater than you can see. All I ask of my children is to live honest and loving lives. When you live this way, you honour me and darkness cannot prevail.

My light is your fortress, your armour. Use it as a shield of protection. Trust in it and you will find peace. I am of the light and the light is of me. When you surround yourself with my light, you are surrounding yourself with me.

My love, children is a stronghold. When you love me and live according to the commandments I have left behind, no enemy can steal you away from me. No one can take the reward that is yours or take your place at my table. I love you.

Find shelter in me. Know that no matter how hard your life is at the moment that I am with you, loving you, my children. Nothing in this life is forever or permanent. The ultimate joy will be found when I call you home to me. Believe in that, trust in that and you will find peace, knowing that no pain is forever.

Protection, shelter, safety can all be found within my light. I am your fortress, your stronghold, your sanctuary. Do not forget this my children, and find refuge in me.

Hold My Hand

You do not need to physically see me to know me, my children. I am here, reach out and hold my hand.

Many of you think of me in terms of a person, lifelike as you are. It is when you humanize me that you cannot hear me; for I do not speak to your ear but to your spirit, your soul. I speak to the very essence of your being.

When you know me through the eyes of your spirit you will understand. You will know that I walk with you all your days and am ever at your side. I will never forsake or abandon you. If I did it would be to abandon myself; for you are me and I of you. You are my child, my creation, my joy and yes, sometimes my sorrow.

You can hold me in your heart, knowing I am there, loving you. In this way you can hold my hand, drawing upon me for support, courage and strength. You can find security and peace within me.

No matter what you do, or what you say, my hand is there, as am I, waiting. If you wander and leave, I will wait. I will wait until the end of days for you to return and to take my hand; to claim me as your own and let my light shine upon and within you.

All you need to do is call my name and seek me out. I will wash away the pain replacing it with love. Know this though, you cannot just say the words with your mouth, you must mean them and speak them from your very soul; the source and light that connects my children to me.

Remember, this too. As a parent holds a child to keep them from straying, I too hold your hand to pull you back and away from unseen dangers. You may not ever know when I gently tug and pull you away from making things worse, or exposing yourself to danger.

If, however you decide to let go of my hand, I will release you. You have the will to decide whether to walk fully with me or walk in darkness. I will always give you the choice to choose light, love and eternal happiness over darkness, pain and sorrow. The choice is yours and yours alone. You just decide whether or not you'll walk with me.

I am here for you my children. Won't you reach out and hold my hand?

Do Not Doubt Me

I am here and I am working on your behalf. Do not doubt me, my children.

I know it is difficult right now and things do not appear to be getting better but I am here. My angels are here and my people are here to guide and assist. They grow in numbers even in their weariness; for though the battle against the enemy is long and hard, my people endure.

These troubles are not of my creation. It is when one strives for power and control over another that these things happen. People who think only of themselves and how to control another have lost their way. They are my children wandering in the dark. Shine your light for them.

The times have been foretold, some to a few and others to many. Use it as an opportunity to spend time with your loved ones, treating them gently and with love and compassion. Strengthen your bonds at this time, do not tear them down or put up walls.

Most of all, pray. Talk to me, come closer to me, hold my hand but do not blame me for the work of the enemy. Do not ask me why I am doing this to you, it is not me. There will be a time when I step into the world again to intervene but that time has not yet come.

Be conscious of your thoughts and actions for they can betray you. They can either brighten or dim your light; the light of the Spirit that resides within is strong. I know all, see all and understand your struggle.

This is a time for you to have courage and faith. It is a time to strengthen your bond with me, not to doubt it. Use your time wisely my children.

I am with you, do not doubt it, do not doubt me.

You Are Unique

There is no other like you, my children, you are unique.

You are wonderfully made, full of goodness and light. Each of you a shining thread, alike and yet different. Though you may look alike, and resemble others, no two are the same.

Each of you has your own wonderful soul. It is a link to me and your light flows to and from me. Take my light and use it. Watch how it grows and strengthens. Don't deny my light. It will lead you to darkness and you will forget just how special and unique you truly are.

Each individual is carrying their own set of talents and strengths. Use your talents for the betterment of this world. Help each other, love each other and hold each other up in times of trouble and sorrow. Draw on each other for strength my children.

Each one of you possesses your own unique personality. It sets you apart from others. Your smile, your sense of humour, the way you react to things, these things are yours and yours alone. Use your smile to brighten another's day, your sense of humour to make someone laugh.

Take pleasure in your uniqueness. Do not try to become like another, be yourself. Don't let others influence you negatively. It is when you lose yourself and stop living with kindness, compassion and love that you forget just how special you are.

I have given each of you a gift that sets you apart from the other. Every one of you has different talents that are required at different times throughout your life and the life of others. Use your gifts for good and they will multiply and bring you great joy.

Never forget, my children, that you are unique and wonderfully made.

Live With Love

Live with love, my children. It is the greatest gift I have given. Make sure you use it often, and wisely.

I have loved you since the beginning. For you, I sent my love to earth; a Son to lead the way and show you how to live, how to forgive, in other words, how to love.

Your gift of love is without limits. You have the capacity to love every person you meet. To greet them with smiles and love in your heart.

Live your life with kindness, understanding and compassion. These are traits based in love. Share yourself with others, helping when needed. Be a friend to the elderly who have no others, to the children who have no parents and to the people who live alone. When you share yourself with them it is an act of love and they see and find me through you.

Many people in this world are in need of love. People who are lonely, disheartened; the poor, the sick, the hungry and the lost all need to know they are not alone in this world. They are my children also, and in need of love, a love which you can provide.

When you show love towards another you are showing your love to me; for what you do unto your brother and sister so you do unto me. When you do not act in love and hurt another, you also hurt me. Everyone is an extension of me, of my love.

There have been many messages, many letters across the ages. I will continue to find messengers to talk to my children. The greatest of all messages, the one repeated most often and in many different ways is to love one another. Love one another as I have loved you.

Do not stow your love away, keeping it behind closed doors, my children. Share it, receive it and believe in it. Love will carry you through.
Live a good life, my children. Choose every day to live with love.

About the Author

Leslie is not only an author, she is also an inspirational blogger and poet. Her posts have been read by people from more than 50 countries around the world.

Leslie has heard God's calling and continues to answer in her works. Her faith is strong and unwavering; engrained in her very fibre. This is her second spiritual book and we expect it will not be her last.

Leslie lives in the serene town of Orillia, Ontario.

Other Books by Leslie

Inspirational / Spiritual

You Were Made to Shine

Children's Rhyming

When You Have the Sniffy Sniffles

Self-Help

Hopes, Dreams and Desires

Website: https://www.lcdobson.ca

Facebook: https://www.facebook.com/ladyl444/

Twitter: https://twitter.com/ladyl444

Instagram: https://instagram.com/dobson4444

Want to see what Leslie's working on next?
Follow her on social media and sign up for her
newsletter at https://lcdobson.ca/sign-me-up

www.ingramcontent.com/pod-product-compliance
Lightning Source LLC
LaVergne TN
LVHW021354080426
835508LV00020B/2275